BIRMINGHAM

A Welcome from the Provost

Welcome to one of the most remarkable cathedrals in England. Birmingham Cathedral is at the centre of the city and reminds us of God at the heart of the creation and the world. Here is a quiet place in a bustling metropolis: a still point in a turning world.

As you come up the Queen's Walk you see the tower with its dome and cupola. Uniquely in England, this is modelled on the central dome of Santa Maria della Salute in Venice which Thomas Archer saw on his travels, a church built in the mid 17th century by Longhena. The walls of the tower are concave and the remarkable movement from square tower to circular dome is covered by elaborate pairs of scrolls, as in Venice. The cupola with its wrought-iron balustrade gives a wonderful view of the whole city. The cathedral is set at a diagonal in The Square emphasising its quality of grace and economy of style. It is now the oldest complete building in Birmingham.

We hope you will enjoy your visit to us, and we ask for God's blessing on you and your family.

From medieval times, the settlement around the centre of Birmingham was served by the ancient and wonderful parish church of St Martin's. Now clad in a 19th-century guise, it conceals at its heart carvings and tombwork dating back to the 12th and 13th centuries.

In the 17th century Birmingham began to grow significantly, yet it was not until 1708, in the reign of Queen Anne, that Birmingham's first new parish since the Middle Ages was created. Fittingly named High Town, the new district stood at the growing city's highest point. The panorama, looking up from St Martin's, was marvellous, with splendid houses – New Hall was one – gracing the hilltop. Before a stone was laid, it was clear that on this site, the new parish church of St Philip would be a major and dominating feature of the cityscape. Such a prestigious commission was not to be entrusted lightly.

The chosen architect was Thomas Archer, a courtier of Queen Anne, whose family estate was at Umberslade Hall, 12 miles from the city. He, like most wealthy young men of the day, had completed his education by undertaking the Grand Tour of Western Europe and in particular of Italy. Of all his experiences at the time, it was the architecture of that country which left the deepest impression, particularly the works of Bernini in Rome. Archer also formed a friendship with the architect Boromini. On his return, Umberslade Hall became the centre of a new, creative approach to architecture. This, no doubt, influenced the commissioning panel for the new parish church.

RIGHT: *Thomas Archer's original church was furnished with beautifully made oak pews with doors and brass fittings, which were removed when the church became a cathedral. These two exquisite door handles are original Queen Anne fittings and can be found on the door at the eastern end of the South Aisle Chapel.*

A CHURCH ON A HILL

ABOVE: *The nave from the west end. The galleries remain as Thomas Archer built them, but the chancel was extended in the 1880s. The art nouveau lighting chandeliers date from around 1905, when St Philip's parish church became Birmingham Cathedral.*

Both the details and the overall plan of St Philip's show elaborate yet simplified forms of the Italian style. In the exterior moulding and stonework is an intriguing blend of ideas, described by Pevsner as 'a rare example of the elusive English Baroque'.

Fittingly, perhaps, it is the tower, with its fluted piers, concave sides and elaborate dome that is the physical and aesthetic high point of one of England's most creative pieces of Baroque architecture.

Birmingham's new parish church of St Philip was consecrated in 1715. Records show that the total cost of building was £5,000. 6s. 4d.

The tower still needed some embellishment and finishing, and an inscription over the door at the main porch records that 'His most excellent Majesty King George, upon the kind application of Sir Richard Gough to the Rt. Hon. Sir Robert Walpole, gave £600 towards finishing the church AD1725'. Gough's family crest, a boar's head, was incorporated into the bronze weathervane on top of the lantern gallery of the dome.

The north and south galleries remain as Thomas Archer built them. Two box pews at the back of the nave remind us of how the whole church must have been originally furnished with beautifully made oak pews with doors and brass fittings. Above the Provost's pew is a remarkable monument to Edward Thomason, maker of medallions in Birmingham by a new process, who sent boxes of his wares to the crowned heads of Europe and reaped many knighthoods and honours. A tablet on one of the north

BELOW: *St Philip's in its early days. The first rectors lived in the fine house second from left in the illustration. Although there were many burials in the city, there were only two churchyards. Consequently, the office of sexton of St Philip's was an important one and competition for the post was great.*

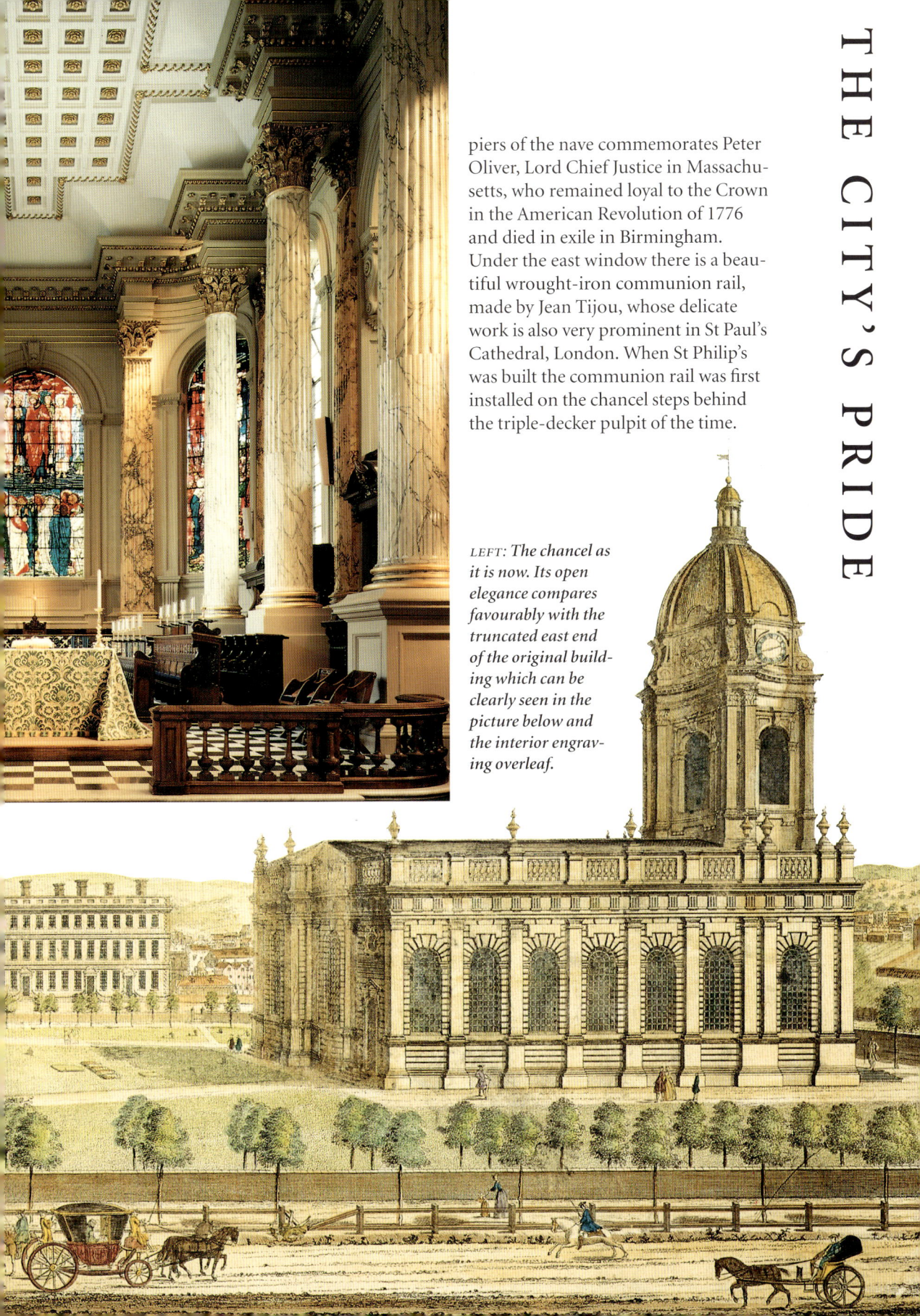

piers of the nave commemorates Peter Oliver, Lord Chief Justice in Massachusetts, who remained loyal to the Crown in the American Revolution of 1776 and died in exile in Birmingham. Under the east window there is a beautiful wrought-iron communion rail, made by Jean Tijou, whose delicate work is also very prominent in St Paul's Cathedral, London. When St Philip's was built the communion rail was first installed on the chancel steps behind the triple-decker pulpit of the time.

LEFT: *The chancel as it is now. Its open elegance compares favourably with the truncated east end of the original building which can be clearly seen in the picture below and the interior engraving overleaf.*

THE CITY'S PRIDE

ABOVE: The interior in 1837, showing the shallow apse, the triple-decker pulpit, and the box pews. The choir and the organ were both situated at the west end. The galleries were original and have survived.

In Archer's original church, the apse at the east end was small, with the choir and organ in a gallery at the west end. The interior was dominated by a huge three-decker pulpit, built high so that the preacher could be seen from the seats at the back of the gallery. The communion table was forced to hide behind it.

Towards the end of the 19th century congregations had grown substantially, and the elevation of St Philip's to cathedral status was becoming a possibility. As a result, the church was enlarged in 1884 by J.A. Chatwin. A new chancel was built at the east end with additional columns, and stalls for choir, archdeacons and canons set in the new space. The organ was installed in its present position on the north side of the new chancel.

Perhaps most significantly for today's cathedral, Miss Emma Chadwick Villiers-Wilkes, an heiress of a

A GROWING CHURCH

wire company, gave money for the installation of three magnificent new east-end windows by the great Pre-Raphaelite artist Sir Edward Burne-Jones, who lived nearby and had been baptised in the church. Later Burne-Jones added a fourth window at the west end. Memorials of the 19th century include the tomb of Samuel Lines, one of the leaders of the Royal Birmingham Society of Artists, which he helped to found and of which he remained Treasurer for over 40 years, until his retirement at the age of 80.

RIGHT AND BELOW: *Two details from the Last Judgement window by Sir Edward Burne-Jones. Christ in majesty raises his hand in blessing, surrounded by archangels and angels holding symbols of keys and incense and the book of life. The people of the world look upwards in fear and distress as the end of the world is revealed.*

The four great windows are in two locations: three at the east end – the Nativity, Ascension and Crucifixion windows – with the great Last Judgement window at the west end.

In the Ascension window (1885) Christ stands within the heavenly realm. Below, the disciples look upwards. Burne-Jones, echoing Michelangelo, has given them a tremendous sense of full-bodiedness compared with the ethereal quality of those above.

In the Nativity window (1887) Virgin and Child are surrounded by Joseph and the angels. A fold encloses the sheep, above which are angels, their wings and faces a curved arc of tremendous power and energy. The three shepherds gaze upwards in a landscape of dark mystery.

In the Crucifixion window (1887) Christ looks down on his Holy Mother. St John looks up in loving adoration. At the foot of the Cross, weeping, is Mary Magdalene, the sinner become saint, surrounded by soldiers with their spears about to pierce.

In the dramatic Last Judgement window (1897) the Archangel Michael sounds his trumpet for the end of the world. A figure on the right represents us, an onlooker stepping forward into the fearful crowd as the city in the background crumbles. Christ is seated at the heart of his angelic community, not triumphant but the humble second person of the Trinity.

LEFT: *The Crucifixion window. Here is no Gothic Christ emaciated, but a victorious figure commending his beloved disciple with authority and power. Mary, at the foot of the cross in blue, and St John, in red and green, look up to Christ as he commits each to the other. St Mary Magdalene kneels at the foot of the cross behind the Blessed Virgin and in an extraordinary way forms a powerful anchor base to the construction of the picture.*

THE BURNE-JONES WINDOWS

LEFT: *The Nativity window expresses the extraordinary sinuous elements in Edward Burne-Jones' work. The curve of the Angelic Host, reflected in the trees and the cave, becomes the curve of the sheep fold. The arched back of Joseph and the curves of the angels all create a tremendous symphony of harmony and order.*

A perfect synergy of worker and artist make this window an important precursor to the Arts and Crafts movement, an aesthetic and social movement of the late 19th century that sprang from a dissatisfaction with the products of industrialism on account of their poor quality and designs. Burne-Jones, from his Oxford days, was a friend of William Morris, whose company lay at the heart of the movement.

The 18th and 19th centuries saw Birmingham become the major manufacturing centre of the British Empire, a 'city of a thousand trades' based on a vast range of metal industries. In 1905, the creation of a separate see under the greatest theologian of the day, Bishop Charles Gore, gave Birmingham true city status and an importance unparalleled in its history.

Other changes took place. The new cathedral entered into the long tradition of Anglican cathedral worship, with the introduction of regular Choral Evensong. This still continues. The Bishop's throne and canons' stalls were set up in the chancel. In the nave, the wonderful old box pews were removed, to be replaced by chairs, and art nouveau chandeliers provided new electric lighting.

During World War II the cathedral was bombed and set ablaze on 7 November 1940. All the windows were destroyed, but fortunately the Burne-Jones glass had already been removed for storage in a mineshaft on the Welsh borders. Roofless and covered with corrugated iron sheeting, the cathedral continued to be a house of prayer throughout the war. This and the subsequent restoration were the heroic work of J.H. Richards, Provost 1937–48, whose house was used constantly by returning servicemen as a place for rest, companionship and refreshment.

In 1989 an undercroft was built, providing much-needed space for a song school, music library and room for seminars and meetings of the cathedral community.

ABOVE AND RIGHT: *The organ (1715) is by Thomas Schwarbrick of Warwick. Its case is original, enlarged and repaired by Snetzler in 1777, rebuilt in 1805 by Pike, relocated in 1883 and enlarged to three manuals by Nicholson of Worcester in 1894. In 1929 Nicholson rebuilt it with four manuals, a modern console and pneumatic action. Although the 1940 bombs did not damage it, it did receive a soaking from an over-zealous fire brigade. It was then stored at Pershore Abbey, returning in 1948. In 1993 Nicholson carried out a major rebuild, made possible by the generosity of the Bigbury Trust.*

A CHURCH TRADITION

RIGHT: *Modern sculpture at its best. Peter Ball of Newark has taken a simple wooden railway sleeper and fashioned it into the cross and figure of Christ crucified. The copper and bronze foil complement the darkness of the wood in presenting a Christ of pathos and suffering yet 'reigning from the tree'.*

At the centre of one of the most cosmopolitan and industrialized cities in Europe, the cathedral has a most important vocation. First, it is a house of prayer: nothing has greater priority than the daily worship of God, both said and sung. We pray every day for the city and its needs, undergirding the outreach ministries to the homeless and the young. Each day, many people bring their thoughts and intercessions from the bustle and noise of the world outside. The cathedral becomes a 'still point' of silence for the city.

Secondly, this church is the 'cathedra' of the Bishop, his throne and seat of ministry. He teaches and preaches here to the many parishes of the diocese which make up the multi-racial city. The cathedral education department continues this work in the city's schools.

Thirdly, the cathedral is the parish church of the city centre, with a special responsibility to the thousands who work nearby and walk past its doors. The Cathedral Square has over 100 companies involved in the financial and commercial sectors of city life. No other cathedral close has the Bank of England as a distinguished neighbour!

Fourthly, the cathedral has, for 300 years, been at the centre of civic life. Before the building of the Town Hall in 1843, St Philip's Church was the main

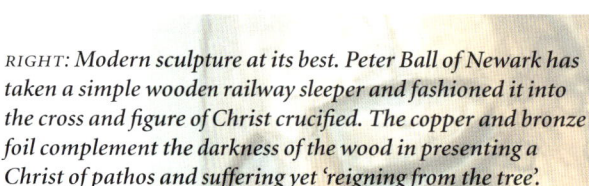

LEFT: *Children's days are held in the cathedral three times a year, usually during the major Christian festivals. There is a strong dramatic tradition with a cycle of Mystery Plays performed every three years.*